ALL IN A DAY'S WORK

Witty, modern poetic verse
on professions, careers
and jobs

Martyn G. Surridge

Published under licence by Brown Dog Books and The Self Publishing Partnership 7 Green Park Station, Bath BA1 1JB

www.selfpublishingpartnership.co.uk

ISBN 978-1-903-05639-4

Cover design by Kevin Rylands

Printed and bound by CPI Group (UK) Ltd, Croydon CR0 4YY

To my family, for all their support.

Contents

Everyday Life: pages 1–66

25. Horologists
26. Jobsworths
27. Ladies' Fashion Designers
28. Landscape Gardeners
29. Librarians
30. Lighthouse Keepers
31. Market Traders
32. Mathematicians
33. Mechanics
34. Meter Readers
35. Nurses
36. Ophthalmic Opticians
37. Osteopaths
38. Painters
39. Painters and Decorators
40. Pathologists
41. Personal Fitness Trainers
42. Personal Secretaries
43. Pest Controllers
44. Photographers
45. Physiotherapists
46. Pilots
47. Plumbers
48. Police Detectives
49. Postmen
50. Removal Men
51. Salesmen
52. Spin Doctors
53. Surgeons
54. Surveyors
55. Taxi Drivers
56. Teachers
57. Telesales Staff
58. Traffic Wardens
59. Travel Agents
60. Used Car Dealers
61. Vets
62. Vicars
63. Waiters and Waitresses

Sporty Types: pages 67–79

Businesslike: pages 80–89

Foreword

I hope the reader will be entertained by reading my publication. It provides a modern-day approach to writing poetic verse that shows the common touch and the humorous side to people's everyday lives in their chosen occupations.

It gives an insight into and understanding of the work of others, and reflects on the thoughts of individual experiences of working for a living in today's society.

Martyn G. Surridge

Everyday Life

1. Actors and Actresses

Ponder the plot
Think through the script
Learn all the lines
Subconsciously, bit by bit

Play the part
Act out the scene
Trust your memory
Down to the timing

Star of the future
Stage, film or TV.
Real-life situations?
Only pretending to be!

Be mindful of others
Be aware of yourself;
Playing out characters
Of someone else

2. Advertising and Marketing Executives

Creativity with psychology in mind
Sensationalises everything through
Clichés, gimmicks, offers and hype
In front of people viewing in prime time
Cleverly devised tricks to trigger
Emotive responses in awareness to buying

Promotional skills, presentation, visuals,
Drumming up ideas working with
A budget to a brief on a timescale,
Thinking and scheming
Seeing is believing,
Promoting regularly on a campaign trail

Glossy literature, powerful words to pictures;
TV advertising put together
With celebrities acting out to endorse
Catchy music to remember
With a persuasive voice
Campaigning and successfully promoting
The brand professionally

3. Air Traffic Controllers

Passengers fly all over the world in
Different time zones through other countries' air space
Traffic controllers control all movement
With safety a priority in performing
Their duties in their own air space

They ensure clear flight paths, safe
Runways to avoid congestion in crowded skies
They guide in, change altitudes, stack
Planes if bad weather comes in
And landing is a danger to lives

They communicate with all pilots, liaise
With ground control to plan every detail,
They train to understand the art of
Maps, grids, computer analysis,
Covering all eventualities with
Experience, knowledge and skills

4. Archaeologists

They live and work in the here and now
They can't put the past behind them somehow
Their minds focus on unearthing ancient history
Forever searching for another life that existed
Left by the unknown to discover
The origin and all its mystery

Playing a patience game: digging, brushing, sifting,
On their knees with endeavour and pain
Searching for any signs or evidence something
Exists in the team dig, working the land and
Every grain of sand that might give answers to
Questions to life of animals and mankind

Digging up bones slowly, not fast,
From inhabitants of the past
Discovering settlements and the
Ways of life of dwellers, they
See dinosaur fossils that once ruled the earth.
With every discovery they will
Analyse, research and number
What they have unearthed

5. Architects

They welcome the challenge of
Designing a project on a plot of land
To be given artistic licence
To be innovative and creative
As they like it, with freedom to do
Their work with a sharp pencil
In their hand

They think out new designs,
Alterations to dwellings of all kinds,
They formulate ideas into drawings
Making best use of dimensions
Light, height and space
With buildings that stand the test of time
To make their mark on the landscape

They stay with the project within the time
Scale brief and budget costs
To observe the work in progress through
All stages of the process
To deliver a building of character
That meets planning regulations
Right up to the completion of the job

6. Auctioneers

Roll up, bring in your hidden treasure!
There's a price on them;
With money at stake
They're cautious in valuations
They decide how much
Money you can make

Wanting to see fine arts
And antiques that excite
And delight the experts,
The buyers decide the
Saleable value
The estimate based on the
Condition and age, from research

The showroom crowded with buyers
Browsing through the items,
Searching for the collectable one,
Checking out the lot number and
The bidding slot, to make sure
There is time to bid on

When the sale gets going
With bids to and fro-ing
Feel the buzz, excitement and sound
Going, going, gone!
Down comes the hammer.
Someone's a lucky winner, outbidding the competition around

7. Beach Lifeguards

Swimmers who ignore the peril of the sea
Look above not beyond the coastline
Lifeguards see with eyes and binoculars
Warning bathers of dangers that can
Can occur any time

People who neglect the flags and warnings
Don't understand the nature and power of the sea,
They see the activity and watch out with intensity
To avoid the risk of injury

The tidal water, the winds, the momentum
Of waves can change quickly
They've done the hard training, swimming the miles
Gaining skills as a lifeguard
Helping out swimmers in extreme difficulty

Jet-skis and speedboats race across the water
Enjoying the water on a hot summer's day,
Accidents can happen; they remain on standby
In emergencies, to rescue and save

8. Bookmakers

Bookmakers are money-makers
Accountants all but in name,
They entice the sporting gamblers
In offering different odds; why they
Play a waiting and percentage game

They see if punters will take the bait
Handing over their stake,
Whoever wins, they make sure of
Profit they will make
The mug punters throw away
Their tickets in the bin,
Having taken a gamble trying
To outsmart them, believing they could win

They lay big bets
To keep liabilities low,
They make up the books
From sources of knowledge
And whispers from people who
Are in the know

They hope outsiders win so
They can clean up and
Pocket the lot; if favourites
Come in they calculate
It all beforehand, taking
A percentage of the pot.
Whatever the odds, whoever wins,
Punters can't get one over the
Bookmakers betting on everything

9. Builders

White van man
One-man bands,
No paper trail
Cash in hand

Rough old estimate
Breaking the law,
In your area
Done it before

Start right away
Another job on,
Got to get off –
Promised someone

Done at last
Sorry about delay,
Let's talk cash
Be on my way.

Hey, wait a minute,
Way over the top.
Did tell you, mate,
I estimated the lot

See you later?
I don't think so!
On your way
You so and so!

10. Butlers

Head manservant: trusted,
Reliable and determined
Maker of the peace
With the staff,
Timekeeper to a routine to keep
The household tidy and clean
Hit the ground running
To avoid complaints coming

White shirt, black tie
Image and respect
To the owners
And their way of life,
Orders and commands
Problems and demands
From the man of the house
And his lady wife

Ready to dine
Dressed up and refined,
Served up professionally,
China plates, crystal glasses,
Silver cutlery
Laid out in line,
Each course on time
Accompanied by wine
The vintage cellar kind

All tasks and duties
All planned – no excuses.
All jobs undertaken
With satisfaction and pride,
Take each day as it comes
Serving others' needs
Dedicated with
Service in mind

11. Call Centre Advisors

It's not their fault
That the client feels
Annoyed and frustrated,
Pressing option buttons
On a system that's automated,
Waiting in a queue
Listening to repeated music
They may hate,
Just to communicate

It seems a long time
To speak online;
Clients understands
The need for security
Checks and personal identification
Important to the company
But the clients pay
The cost to get
The information

They're here to help
To answer any questions,
Resolve any problems,
Make positive suggestions.
They do their best
To satisfy clients' needs
With best customer advice
They hope it's
What you believe.

12. Carpenters

Carpenters are masters
In making good with wood
Applying their trade to building up structures
Adding skills, the finishing touches
Where woodwork is to be done or made

They build it, join it
Carve and shape it,
Plane smooth, glue or nail it
Leaving for painters to paint and preserve it
To finish the work on it

They build, join and install new
Kitchens, staircases in the hall,
Working on the rooftops
Creating space and a view,
Doing a conversion room
In the loft

All familiar with names
The soft and hard wood grains
Some specialise in making furniture
Others share skills on the job
With sparkies, spreadies and brickies
They are known as chippies

13. Chefs

A day in the life
Of a humble chef,
He often aspires
To become the very best

Every day he hopes
To become a master,
Avoiding the pitfalls
And presentational disaster

Everything is planned
To a joy on a plate,
Cooked to perfection
Tasting and smelling great

Everyone's eyes down
Looking at the menu,
A special occasion, maybe,
A cosy eating-out venue

Satisfied all the diners?
Chef takes a bow.
Food for thought,
If only we knew how

14. Chiropodists

Other professions look after
Your mind, your money,
Your needs, your body
That's fine!
They look after tired and weary feet
That needs caring attention sometimes

Your feet tell all
About you, the life
You lead, the things
You do
The daily wear and tear we tend to
Put our feet through

The bunions
That look like onions,
The corns
That irritate,
Not forgetting
The hard skin, the
In-growing toenails
That we professionals
Help to eradicate

15. Cleaners

It hides in nooks and crannies
Sunshine makes it appear,
Out come the cleaners
Dust and cobwebs disappear

They confess to be possessed
With minor particles in the air,
The cleaners won't have them
Lying about anywhere

They don't shirk work
However hard,
Wearing out
Their knees and arms
From the moment they start

All done and dusted
All spick and span,
Love doing it
To remove it
With hoover, brush and pan

All neat and tidy
No bugs or germs to be seen,
All clean and pristine
Where the cleaners have been.

16. Dentists

Filling, drilling
Probing, digging
Under a bright light.
A comfy chair,
A word here and there,
Trusting everything is right

A bridge too far
A root so deep;
Crown it all
To save our teeth

A dentist prevents decay
Skilled and highly trained;
Reducing our anxiety
Removing our pain

17. Dog Trainers

Those disobedient pets that might have bitten
Other dogs or their vets,
They're off to the dog trainers!
Owners claim it's all about antisocial behaviour

They bark out orders, get them into a routine
With some fun and play,
Different breeds have different temperaments
But they still have to learn to behave

There's the untrained puppy dogs – excitable, uncontrollable,
Out to discover
A new world and family, they have to
Be trained and praised to act sensibly and sociably

Learning to heel, stay and lie down
Retraining them when walking around
Progressing to be obedient on their own
Responding to commands to come back alone

Dogs react to the sound of whistles
And respond to their name.
Show patience and give authority; they'll
Be a happy dog because they were well trained

The owner is the master of the dog
Is a family friend living with them?
With lots of exercise, food and discipline
They'll be contented and obey then

18. Driving Instructors

Think how unlucky they are
When you sign up for lessons
And jump into the car

You put their lives at risk
You test their patience
How many lessons, did you insist?

No knowledge, experience or foot control
No idea of directions to go
Lucky they have dual control

Panic sets in when the gear's selected
The first lesson is all about gaining
Trust and getting connected

Bump, jump, feeling a fool
No emotions, please, it's a long haul;
You have to remain calm and cool

Watch the dog cross the road
Watch the lorry with the load,
Watch, there's a roundabout ahead
Slow down, the traffic light's red

Pull over now –
It's been a scary journey
Never mind. Next time
You'll be more experienced
And less wary

19. Electricians

Whether they repair or install
They can't afford to make mistakes,
They have to be on the ball
To concentrate where safety is at stake.
That's how it works,
Doing electrical work

It's essential to know all about
Diagrams, rules and regulations,
The correct wiring and the colour
Codes to use before repairs and installation –
There are no shortcuts
In wiring things up

They light up the dark,
Link up to the mains
Keep the power going?
To the socket for the appliances
To be working again,
They are the electrical brains
'Sparky' is their trade name

20. Farmhands

They don't boast
When folk say
They are harder-working than most,
All hands to the task
All down to hard graft
Dawn to dusk

Some folk say
They're the salt of the earth,
Working outside all day.
A labour of love,
Putting it all together
In all weathers

Spring newborns,
Hours with cows
Harvesting wheat and corn,
It's all worthwhile
By a country mile
Labouring on a farm

21. Gardeners

Welcome to my garden
It's my domain
In my own world where I prefer to remain.
Up early in the morning
Done by twilight
I tidy up, prune and cut, in tranquil delight

My garden's round and flat ground
It's my own plot where I can landscape
And cultivate my lot.
I feed, I water,
Through summer to autumn,
I put life into seeds
Which grow into leaves,
I get down on my knees
To remove all those weeds

Time to sit back and relax in my chair
Let nature do its work while I admire
The fruit and flowers that they bear

My garden is my heaven
It's all taken shape,
It changes all seasons
It's my escape

22. GPs

How're you feeling?
Sorry I'm late
I have to say, doc,
Not very great

Got pains in my back,
Pulses in my head,
Pains in my joints,
I fell out of bed.

Got tingling in my ears,
Got a gippy tummy,
Got blisters on my feet –
It isn't very funny.

My daughter's got pregnant
My son's run away,
I've still got constipation
It won't go away.

It's all about getting older.
Keep taking the pills –
Exactly what the doctor ordered
Sorry about your ills.

Keep the bones moving
Keep the mind clear,
Maybe next appointment
You won't keep bending my ear

23. Grooms

There's always room for a good groom
Working in a racing stable
Up early, getting the horses up, clearing the mess up
Grooming them ready for training exercises
Off to the races to win owners prizes

There's always a need for a good groom
Working on a stud farm
Helping hands, horses that need feeding, tack that needs
cleaning
Grooming them ready for the act of breeding
For the mares to be conceiving

There's always a place for a good groom
In a family-run estate
Riding out, keeping the horses fit, cleaning the kit
Grooming for the owners
To ride out at their leisure
In the country for their pleasure

24. Hairdressers

Wash it out,
Snip a bit off here
Flick it about there,
Cut and shape the hair
Hairstyle is new!
Matches your dress, hat and shoes

Chit and chat
About this and that,
Going somewhere on a date,
Going out with a mate
Or out with someone special?
For a reason to celebrate!

Like the shape and cut?
Like the style with it up?
Matches your face and eyes.
If there's a wind outside
It could spoil the surprise

25. Horologists

They can set time in motion
Build mechanisms for standing up
Clocks or wristwatches,
They can make time a quiet time
Without hearing the sound of tick-tock

They can repair replicate movements
Wind forward, turn back time,
Make it stop!
With the skills of their hands and eye
And precision instruments, the
Clock makers' stock

The world revolves
Around accurate time,
People like jewelled designs
For keeping a long time
Face, hands and numbers you see
Their masterwork is hidden inside
Ticking away
Quietly and reliably

With the power of batteries, electricity
And the old winding-up way
It triggers all moving parts
To give an exact measurement of
Time by the minute, hour and day

26. Jobsworths

Could be a government official
A suit and tie, a uniformed man
Some badged-up jumped-up individual
Rules and regulations waving in his hands
Bossing the point, laying down the law,
A jobsworth creates more problems than before

Not for complaining to, reasoning
Or changing, only toeing the line;
On a power trip, making people's lives
A misery without even trying,
Taking the flak, driving the public insane
Politically correct yet inflexible all the same

Standing his ground,
Shouting orders out, important he sounds.
Final words, spoken rules can't be broken
However absurd, they must be observed
Jobsworth not popular in his work,
No common sense when carrying out chapter and verse

27. Ladies' Fashion Designers

It's down to them to inspire
With flair and imagination,
Designing original fashionable clothes
Seen on the catwalk
That become a marketing sensation.
Creating a trend with a designer
Label to appeal to all the buyers,
To look pleasing to the eye
To try on the clothes to want to buy

The drawings, the shapes,
Forever exploring
The ideas with materials,
To match the colours decided.
The tight fit, the loose fit,
The long and short bit,
The classic ladies' style
The young and trendy
In for a while,
To all new seasons
For all to see
Creating style, image and colours
To match all accessories

28. Landscape Gardeners

Seeking out space
To articulately design and create
From ideas to a computer image.
Country gardens, modern trends,
A garden landscape from start to end

A plot of land
To cultivate by hand:
Soil to prepare the ground for digging
Planting trees, flowers, shrubs to bring
Life into a garden for a new beginning

It's their domain
Where they will remain,
They have a part to play to improve
The display, to tidy everything
Along the way

Nature takes over
Fast-growing or slower: picture the
Scene: weathers and seasons intervene,
Fruit and flowers appear
All from a landscape gardener's skills and ideas

29. Librarians

It's a bookworm's delight
All peaceful and quiet,
A room where you can
Hear a pin drop.
Pick up a book, sign it out
And return them
When your time's up

Books of fact or fiction,
Old books, revised editions,
They'll point you in the direction
Of your preferred reading section,
Or reference the computer
To authors' entire works
Or answer any questions

Pick and choose your book
Casual or serious? Look
For knowledge, or about
Someone's life murder, or romance?
You decide.
The library provides.
The librarian helps you
If you need to confide.

30. Lighthouse Keepers

All alone, on their own,
Surrounded by waves
And the sounds of the sea,
A beacon light shines
Bright over my head
To warn ships of the
Dangers of the sea

The home is a lighthouse
The job is to look out
To keep the lights on;
To warn and guide
The ships at night
To the dangers both
Far and wide

They welcome the company
Of strangers, who bring out
Fresh supplies for them.
They are left alone
To fend and command
The light to bring ships
Home safely in the
Darkest nights

31. Market Traders

They buy to sell at a profit
To earn a decent living,
Up at the crack of dawn
To make business decisions

To get all the attention
They shout our message out loud
Above the noise and the
Hustle and bustle of the crowd

Their cheeky, corny jokes
Ladies, we love them all
They turn on the old charm
To sell goods on their stall

They are wheeler-dealers
With the gift of the gab,
They must sell to onlookers
To be competitive with
Other market lads

Their life to trade
To barter all their stock,
Up to the end
Of the day
To get rid of the lot

32. Mathematicians

Mathematical geniuses
As they are perceived as
High IQs of the human race
Brain-waving ideas to find scientific
Answers through numbers,
Quantity and space

Mere mortals
Without the mental capacity
Or ability to problem-solve,
Short on logic on the subject
Best left to those who know
How to resolve

Mathematicians of the past
Left a legacy to last;
Seeing now what they discovered then
Formulas written down,
Proof of what they found,
Life then changed direction

Mathematicians of the present,
Learn from the past
For future benefit.
Calculating with equations and symbols
An academic bunch
Who number-crunch
Theorising to test
Their intelligence

33. Mechanics

Working on cars of the past –
Been around, made to last –
Replacing and fitting the old parts
Because owners won't give up on
Them or put them out to grass

Working on cars of the future
All linked up to the computer,
Pressing buttons to not inconvenience you
Technology will never replace mechanics
With their labour and skills, they
Understand dynamics

They get cars started, keep them running,
Tune them up if they sound funny
With high-tech equipment
They can diagnose and fix it,
For road safety and reliability
When drivers are in it

34. Meter Readers

Get started early
Finish late,
Can't stop the dog barking
Who's locked the gate?

It's all about running around
Sometimes feeling fed up and bored,
I'm not popular; all I want is a
Few minutes, a few numbers to record

Why does everyone hide away
When I arrive? Trying to ignore,
All I said is 'I'd like to come in,'
Get out and close the door!

If only things
Were easier.
I'm not demanding money
I'm only a meter reader.

35. Nurses

Sisters bark orders
Organised in chaos,
Patients have needs
Not knowing what day it is

Doctors do demand
Emergencies keep coming,
Tired old feet
Hit the ground running

Charts to read
Paperwork to evaluate,
All about patient care
Hourly checks to make

Early morning
Late shifts,
Someone's been saved
Others sadly miss

Done their bit
Off home to bed,
Recharge the batteries
Nursing themselves instead

36. Ophthalmic Opticians

They invite people to
Come and see them
For full eye tests
Not just to create
Spectacles
But to ensure they see the best

They meet them
Face to face
Testing fading sight
Making close contact
Eye to eye
To see the world in a different light

They prescribe for
Any corrections,
They find they're
Own style and image,
Young or old
Short- or long-sighted
Clear vision is our business

Seeing is believing
There's a world out
There to explore

Reading and writing
They can see things
Better than before.

37. Osteopaths

When the spinal cord
Is out of line
The specialists have a trick
To manipulate your bones
Until you hear a clickety-click

When your neck
Is aching
They know the vital points,
To ease the pain
And free up the joints

There are hundreds of bones
Supported by muscles,
Working all the time
From feet to head
They must be aligned

Bones are fragile,
Bodies do wear,
With the art of
Skilful hand movements
They correct postures
For overwhelming improvement.

38. Painters

The canvas is blank
The paintbrushes are dry,
The artist's impression
Can be seen in the vision:
They paint what they see with their eye

They capture the moment
In portrait or landscape,
Infinite details
All shapes and colours,
For art lovers to admire and appreciate

Their hands are their guide;
Time has no place.
Their finished picture
Tells a story of fine art,
Creating something unique
Never to replicate

39. Painters and Decorators

Painters and decorators
Are never in a rush.
It's the nature of their work
To handle everything purposefully
With their paint and brush

Preparing smooth surfaces,
Undercoating all the time,
Shaping up things to come
To eventually cover up
All the past work that's hidden behind

Every brush-stroke flows
With precision and direction,
Knowing which way to go;
\removing all the blemishes
To a finish that's perfection

Cosy, light rooms
Fresh and vibrant colours,
All down to personal choice,
To match the décor
Of the furnishings complementing each other

40. Pathologists

People die naturally
People die accidentally
People die mysteriously
People die violently

They live their working lives
Finding out the reason why
People die; that's why
They carry out an autopsy
In a high-tech laboratory
To establish the cause and effect
Using their knowledge, skills and
Intelligence, with the aid of
Medical and scientific evidence

They photograph and document,
Analyse all bloods, examining
Organs inside to determine
Why that person died
In suspicious circumstances.
They pass on their findings
To a coroner who will hold
A public inquest
To explain what happened
And establish officially
What caused the death.

41. Personal Fitness Trainers

They have their work cut out:
If clients have never
Before worked out,
They need to get them
Motivated and moving about.
Those who have never
Exercised regularly
Could gain weight
End up losing their
Mobility and energy

They work them to
A planned routine,
Jogging and running a bit,
In the gym getting fit,
Making them puff and pant;
Exhausted, until there's no
Gas left in the tank.
Controlling their diet and
Weight with the
Correct food intake

Strengthening up the muscles
Building up the stamina
Loosening up the joints:
Daily exercises to follow.
To reach goals to earn points,
That's their aim,
Helping others to get there
Remain fit and healthy
Energised again

42. Personal Secretaries

There's more to them than serving up
Refreshments of tea and coffee.
They handle the post
They're the client's host
To ensure business meetings
Run professionally

They're determined and firm in
Arranging diary meetings with the boss.
They control the itinerary
To play his golf
And lunch out in his favourite spot

They say nothing and do everything
Always thinking on their feet,
Known for being trustworthy and reliable
In business matters,
They remain completely discreet

They are cool and composed
If the boss has a crisis day,
They are the secretary:
They do what's necessary
To smooth out the working day

43. Pest Controllers

It's funny to be so popular
In the services they offer
People ring in when panic sets in
They are a problem-solver, pest controller,
Doing a job that people feel uncomfortable watching

The vermin are very disturbing
If the public ignore them
And they get out of control,
It's their business being nosy and suspicious
Looking for evidence of a run
Or a borrowed hole

Some people leave food lying around,
Feeding wildlife too close to the ground.
Laying bait and traps in the best
Place to catch the bees, wasps,
Mice and rats

They get into sheds
They get into roofs
They can get into your head
When they are running loose.
With bait and traps
They keep coming back
To reduce the population
To avoid total infestation

44. Photographers

They are careful and deliberate in the decisions they make
With the camera, the light and the background
For the pictures they take.
They see a vision with a bird's eye view to capture
A moment on the camera that can be viewed by you

They picture this and picture that before they snap
They have to be technical to be professional, focusing
Their minds to react,
Producing images that are natural – as the camera never lies.
A snap becomes a photograph taken instantly
Before it flashes by

They line up different angles, take lots of shots
With processing to come, they can highlight
And select the best of the lot

Landscapes, places, laughing faces to look upon
They bring life into photos that tell stories
Recording a life of memories
For someone

45. Physiotherapists

If you enjoy an active sporting life
You can still pull or tweak something
If your muscles haven't been
Warmed up right,
When the pain and discomfort become extreme
You may need professional help
To treat the body to heal the injury

If you've been working on the body too much
They examine and find the troubled spot,
Introduce exercises for you to do
Working on muscular movements;
Twisting, prodding, stretching
To ease the discomfort;
Giving movement back to you

Some injuries take longer
Than others to heal,
They need special exercises
On a regular basis with a few pills,
There are lessons to be learned if
You carry a few niggles; it's
Best to respond to your body
And rest it up a little

46. Pilots

A pilot is seen as a god in the sky
Points you in the right direction
Wears a smart uniform and tie

Glides through clouds, flies over oceans
Never panics in any situations
Never shows any emotions

Takes you around the world
Lands you on a spot,
Avoids all the turbulence
Steers manually on autopilot

Remains calm and confident
Holds lives in his hands,
Talks about the weather
The altitude and the time he lands

Flights all over
Passengers long gone,
Captain's logged off
And on to another one

47. Plumbers

Their job is
To go with the flow,
Make sure things
Don't get bunged up,
Stop and never go

Their work is
To bend pipes,
Fitting and replacing,
Down and dirty
Where spiders hide
And cobwebs are clinging

Their work involves
Checking
And testing,
Meeting regulations
And standards,
Leak-free, total safety,
Taps, loos, central heating

Their work diagnoses all faults
By regular servicing,
Cuts out all the hassle
And despair in call-out emergencies

48. Police Detectives

It's all about evidence
In a crime scene
Pictures to take
Evidence to collate
Surveying the scene
Searching out clues
Who's done what, how and where to whom

It takes time
To solve a crime
Scientific work
The legwork
The teamwork
Leads to investigate
Gather intelligence, decisions to make

It's all about facts
To make a catch
Question all witnesses
Record all interviews
Take down statements
Narrow down suspects
Find the culprit, check the facts, then arrest
All right, sunshine, now you're mine
The handcuffs click and we are off
To the nick

49. Postmen

Early-morning light
Half-asleep, overloaded bike
Letters and parcels
No return,
Deliver it some time
Got energy to burn

Been here yesterday
Going there today,
Round and round
In circles
Which way anyway?

Letters landing on the mat
Missed the dog!
Junk mail
All recycled back

Tired and exhausted
Home in the rain,
Got to do it again tomorrow
All over again.

50. Removal Men

People up sticks to move to a new home
To start a new life in another postcode
They are around to ensure that, on the day
Of loading, they get there on time to pack
Ready to get going

Boxes galore from ceilings to floor
Up in the loft there are even more,
People pack everything to take away,
Off to another loft, maybe, to put
Out of the way or with furniture on display

They have done all the loading, the
Rubbish has been dumped that's not going,
Arriving at the destination to discover
The heavens have opened and
There's a car parked blocking the driveway

They find an empty shell, fingers pointing out
To put it here, take it there, it's really hard to tell
Tradesmen all over taking up the space
Pandemonium with the kids and the
Pets running all over the place

All done – hard work, taken some hours;
The planning and preparation
The moving and settling down,
But they know how.
Nothing damaged, nothing broken,
Everything out of the truck
On the way, wishing them good luck

51. Salesmen

Spins you a yarn
Weaves you into a web,
Turns on the charm offensive
You're easily led

Loves all that money
Knows the power of words,
Baffles you with technical terms
You've never ever heard

Eventually weakens your resistance
Bores you into submission,
It's all in your best interests
No time for indecision!

Signing on the dotted line
You've conceded, and
Believed it's
What you wanted all the time

52. Spin Doctors

Neither a doctor nor scientist
But on a limited client list
They're a brand of individuals
Politically hard-nosed thinkers
Smooth-talking enthusiastic spinners
A spokesman for others
Talking point for the media to know
That diffuses situations
To maintain the status quo

They find a way
In the game they play
To put out a message
In a favourable way
To make plain a meaning and belief
Down to politically correct words
That are accurate and discreet
All thought out, scripted meticulously
To speak out articulately

53. Surgeons

Precision decision
Heaven knows
What lies ahead

The strength of a lion
The steadiness in the hand
The coolness in the head

Heartbeat: life back
The opening of the eyes

The skill of a human
The weight of expectation
The genius in disguise

54. Surveyors

Buying a property, measuring and
Mapping out a piece of land
Requires the expertise of a surveyor
To accurately report their findings
To see if it is sound as a pound

There's always wear and tear,
Some in a state of disrepair.
Closer inspection reveals all conditions
Clients have to be made aware
What to remedy, when to repair
So they can make decisions

Evidence of damp in walls,
The state of the woodwork,
The pointing in the brickwork,
Cracks in the plaster that
Might reveal a subsistence disaster,
Leading to foundation digging and underpinning

All electrics and plumbing
Down to other tradesmen coming,
They look in drains;
At the state of the window frames;
Woodworm or dry rot?
The condition of the roof
In the loft

Writing a report
With a breakdown of all faults,
Providing an insurance valuation
For the cost of rebuilding the plot
If a fire occurs and destroys the lot

55. Taxi Drivers

Taxi drivers
Queue up in
The rank,
Some erratic drivers
You wouldn't thank,
Always in a hurry
To earn some money,
Off to the pub
Airport run
Nightclub
To have some fun

The meter's ticking
Even before the
Journey's begun,
They avoid the
Congestion by mapping
Out the direction.
Might find yourself
In a jam;
There's always a bus
But you might have to stand

End of journey;
The meter stops
You have to trust the clock.
What it costs:
Add on the tip,
Keep the change,
Back to the bank
Unless waved down
On the way.

56. Teachers

When the school bell tolls
The day of learning unfolds,
Lessons around the classroom begin
All turned up and listening in

Some are clever in the head
Others have heads in the clouds,
Some don't concentrate on their work
Others unruly in school hours

Their enthusiasm inspires to educate
Help them focus on a dream,
Not to lecture or separate
To keep them in the mainstream

Extra help for those who can't cope
With hands-on personal tuition,
Finding an easy way to learn
To encourage confidence and ambition

Their skills implant knowledge and wisdom
Their guidance gives a chance to succeed,
Achieving a higher education
Towards the jobs they need

57. Telesales Staff

Numbers and name games
Tough made appointments
Hard sales gains
All alone
On their own
Motivated on the phone,
Catching people in
To listen in.
Faces unknown
Trying to be convincing,
Selling a service
Or product
To do business

Ready-made scripts
Contacts hit and miss
Tried and tested approach
Keep hitting the list.
Never taken back
By setbacks,
Overcoming objections
Asking questions,
Being persistent
Professional with it.
Telesales:
The hardest form of
Cold-call selling

58. Traffic Wardens

They prowl the street
In broad daylight,
Sneaking up and pouncing
On motorists if their cars
Aren't parked right

They give out tickets
Every minute of the day,
Armed with hand cameras
They stalk and catch their prey

Woe betide you
If the meter stops!
Get you,
You traffic violator,
If you ignore the clock

Let's be having you;
You're breaking the law;
It's raising revenue –
Out come excuses galore

Move on, sir, no abuse:
That's the position.
The fines you pay
Are lawful decisions.

59. Travel Agents

There comes a day when
People like to get away
Wanting to spend their cash
On holidays, to explore or take
Time out to relax

They dream about exotic locations
Cruising, sporting or adventure holidays
Taking in the scenery; out to have fun
Bathing on the beaches, relaxing
Under the sun

Choosing the most suitable brochure
To look their options over
They book and arrange, checking
The dates if available in hotels,
Boats, trains and planes

If travelling in a party
Or going away alone,
They fit in the itinerary
Because they have done the research
As the reps have been there first

From January to December
In hot or cold climates
They can supply all holiday destinations
Handling all the arrangements
To provide the tickets and documentation

60. Used Car Dealers

They try to do their trading,
Selling used cars
Wheeling and dealing.
They're no different to other businesses
They have to make money
On sales, moving cars
It's their living!

They try to build up a
Good reputation, so people can
Buy into their name
They offer choices of models and colours
And sizes on the forecourt –
It's a hard old game!

To be honest, they know little
About past owners or the
Mileage on the clock, then
There's the wear and tear of
The engine: will it run nice and smooth
Or blow up?

They'll promise if you
Show the money
They'll hand over the log
Book, MOT and keys,
It will look better
Than it's worth
And if you're lucky
There's a written guarantee!

61. Vets

If you're an animal lover
And care for your favourite pet
You bet some time, in their lifetime
Their owners will bring them along to the surgery
Seeking help from the vet

They are animal doctors and surgeons
All rolled up into one
The surgery's full of wild and friendly
Animals suffering from illness
Waiting for examination and treatment to be done

All different animals sitting next
To each other, it resembles Noah's ark
Some rare visitors, some strange noises heard
You hear not so familiar sounds
Even in a woodland park

Every day is a hectic day
As they try to heal and care,
Would not want it any other way
Looking after animals' health and fitness
Is their chosen life and career

62. Vicars

Serving the parish
As best they can,
With a book of
Wise words
They believe in
And hold in their hand

They wear collars
Around their neck
And a white frock
As a symbol of religion and teaching
That's recognised
Among the flock

Socialising with the parishioners
Attending garden fetes,
Working with schools
And charities,
Drinking tea and eating
Homemade cakes

Giving hope and help is their intention,
Not divine intervention,
Conducting blessings for funerals
And christenings; joining lives
Together in matrimony

Giving support to all
In the community,
Giving sermons in church,
Reading out chapter and verse
Preaching the faith to all spiritually

63. Waiters and Waitresses

It's not their fault that customers
Sometimes have to wait,
It's down to the diners
Who turn up in great numbers
Waiting for the food, because it's great!

They do make some mistakes
Especially with a busy intake,
Backwards and forwards
Taking orders, carrying plates
Hard on the feet with tables of eight

People can fuss when ordering steak or fish
As the main dish,
Hard to get it right.
Some say though, 'Just as I like it!'

Trying their very best
Serving everything up on request,
Sometimes there's nothing left.
Taking the brunt of the criticism
When it's down to the chef

Finally, the end of the day:
Clear plates; new tables to lay
Appreciate the departing tip
To top up our wages
Just a bit

64. Weather Forecasters

Whatever the weather
They can't always be right!
It can change in the morning
Without warning, then the afternoon
Can turn out sunny and bright

Forecasting 'mainly cloudy with patchy rain'
Could end up in a torrential downpour
It's not an exact science,
Computers are an alliance,
It can make forecasters into fools

Planning a wedding day, a holiday,
Attending an outdoor event?
In summarising the weather on a certain day
They rely on winds, charts and
Pictures that the satellite sent

Rain, snow, ice, fog, heat-wave,
The Met Office puts out daily news.
Wind blows from all directions;
Predicting British weather –
A nightmare for forecasters to do!

65. Writers

Writers are the inspirational kind,
Words are their deeds,
Stimulation comes from their creative minds

Thinking out loud
Imagining all plots,
Writing everything down
To forget it not

The pen is the keyboard;
Computers record
The completed manuscript
Edited ready to submit

Devoted to words
Flowing with meaning,
Open to readers
The written work
For reading

Sporty types

1. Basketball Players

Leaps like a salmon
Tall as a giraffe
No place for shorties
Playing a physical game of basketball
On the boards that are hard

Slide of the hand
Showboating with skill and control
Bouncing ball in all directions
To keep possession
Looking for space to move forward
To pass the ball

On the deck
In the air
Hands waving in despair
Over the head
Under the leg
Score off the backboard
Or straight through the net

Niggly 'stop and go' fouls
Time out given
For changes allowed,
Coach out to motivate
Players, in to take a
Break with energy drinks intake

Shoot on the attack
Other teams on
The counter-attack hit back
Who scores most baskets?
Who takes most chances?
Whose energy lasted?
They win most matches

2. Cricketers

Funny old game!   Strange old names!

A maiden coming over
From cow corner, caught up in the slips.
Legs are short, long, square and fine
LBW out in line.

No balls, wide balls
Long on, long off,
Yorkers and bouncers
Bats and pads,
Umpire's fingers held aloft

Swinging and seaming
Under cloudy skies,
Spinning and scheming
LBW – it's in line

Stumped by the keeper
Trying to hit a six,
Was it a googly,
The wrong 'un or
Was it a mishit?

Bags of wickets
Tons of runs,
Rainy old days.
Duckworth Lewis
Decides the outcome

In a hurry
To the pavilion,
Via the gully
The covers coming on.

'What's the point?'
Says the third man,
Watching the rain
Waiting for the sun.

3. Darts Players

Imagine a dartboard, a jumbled-up clock
No face, no time, no tick or tock
Think of a number, double it, treble it, add it up in your head.
To reach a checkout score
You have to stay one think ahead.

Stand at the ockey, steady hand, beady eye
Watch the flighty darts; fly to the bull's eye
Three in a bed: one hundred and eighty!
Nine darts for starters
Win the legs and sets,
Make the crowd go crazy

Finish up with a winning double
The final shot out to avoid trouble.
Step back, take time, aim –
Making sure the shot counts.
Throw the combination number
Game, set and match:
Knock your opponent out.

4. Fishermen

Five o'clock in the morning
Raining and dark outside,
Time to get the live bait ready
To win a prize

Driving down the empty road
Thinking of the mighty catch,
Hope it won't be a tiddler
To have to keep throwing back!

Arriving at the river bed
Looking for the best place,
Get my tackle ready
I hope they like the taste

Thinking of moving on
Maybe try another bait,
Then suddenly one's on the line
My reputation's at stake!

Reel in on the hook
Pleasantly surprised,
What a whopper I've got!
I've landed the big prize.

Up to win the trophy
The catch is on the scales,
It's really that big –
No need to tell tales.

5. Footballers

Brains in the feet
Balls in the air,
Rough and tough tackles
Flying about everywhere

Wannabe model girls
Flashy sports cars,
Boys' games and toys
Branded superstars

Team game players
Individual winners,
Long-term contracts
Saints or sinners?

Millionaire-style homes
Country Life ways,
Out of the public eye
Until big match days

Early in retirement
Pots of dosh,
A charmed life
With the rich and posh

Back on TV
Back in tracksuits,
Back in the limelight
Without football boots.

6. Golfers

Up on the leaderboard
Down the back nine
Time to put a show on
Put the skills on the line

Practice makes perfect
Missing rough, bunkers and trees
Flying with the eagles
Floating on the breeze

Irons, wedges, drivers
Birdies for a start
Searching for a hole in one
Luck or fine art?

Close to the flag
Putter steady, in control
Down the ball gently rolls
Into the hole

Top of the leaderboard
Well under par
Round of the day
Tells you who you are

7. Jockeys

We may seem younger than we are
Weighing nothing at all,
Wearing shiny bright silks
Horses make us look small

We are a riding machine
Full of thrills and spills,
A professional jockey in the sport
Riding bends and up hills

We ride out early
With a snack intake
We sweat it out in the sauna
To reach the right riding weight

We ride up with the pace
To get into the race –
We are tough as they come
When the horse won't run

With a push and a shove
Getting into the lead,
For money or love
Found the right distance and speed

You win some
You lose some;
Photo finish at the post.
The winner's enclosure
The place to be –
What jockeys want most.

8. Rugby Players

No game for anger, no place to shirk,
No time for egos – all down to physical
Effort, mental skills and teamwork

Strength of a lion, built like an ox,
If you are lean and mean and a running
Machine, you can outrun the lot

Players have their roles, referees have their names
They all make decisions advancing forward
Or defensive duties against each other's game

Jumping up in the line-up, grunts and
Shoving in the scrum,
Power and touch in the forward
Movement on the run

Rules and regulations; players' patience wearing thin
They get punished for all infringements
And can be sent to the sin bin

Cauliflower ear, a squashed nose,
Running with an oval ball;
As the game goes it's:
Who tries to get a try?
Who kicks the most goals?

9. Snooker Players

Walking round and round
Bending up and down,
Moving side to side
With elbows held high

Battle on the table
Colourful scenes,
Chess-like moves
Balls running along the green

Chalky tip cues
White ball on a spot,
Cushions to bounce off
Topsy-turvy screw shot

Drawn-out frames
Boring old draws,
Maximum break is on
Applause from the floor

Pot reds to pockets
Aiming for a ton,
Starting with the yellow ball
Ending on the black one

Off the inside pocket
In off another,
The rub of the green
Wins more frames than the other.

10. Tennis Players

The crowd queue in anticipation
Centre Court's the destination
Players enter to an ovation
There is no love lost
When the umpire calls the toss

Clay, grass and hard courts
Love – not zero or nought
Daddy long legs, windmill arms
Covers all the court
Giving you a better chance

Supreme athletes, mobile feet
Strong minds ready to compete
Playing their own brand
Rackets held in one or two hands

Match underway, no rain delay
The counter-puncher, the front runner.
Working up a sweat; first up
To volley at the net

Point after point, see-sawing,
Crowd on their feet, enjoying
Solid as a rock variety of shot
Angles and space exploring

Top spins, slices, passing shots
Powerful ground strokes, showing off
The skill of the game
The seeded name wants the glory and fame

Who dares win?
To remain focused and able
To sense it, believe it, achieve it
Mentally strong to show they're capable

Who wins key points?
Who makes fewer mistakes?
Who hold serves, who breaks,
Who has match points?
Celebrating with handshakes.

Businesslike

1. Accountants

Figures everything out
Tidy organised mind,
Compiles all sorts
Of financial transactions,
Meets tax deadlines

Backbone of business
Profit and loss calculators,
Sophisticated number-crunchers
Forefront of decision-makers

Paperwork piling up
Data to input,
Spreadsheets for analysis
Producing company reports

Budget change amendments
Alterations to client base,
Taxation for implementation
To final accounts date

2. Bankers

To be honest and frank
It's hard to understand
The workings of a bank

Takes your money
Pays your bills
Changes the earth
Lets you queue at the tills

A faceless service:
Get yourself on line!
Pays little interest;
Makes vast profits
All the time

Trusting your money
To be secure and safe,
Bailed out by us,
The taxpayer:
Utter disgrace

Customer-friendly service
Going, soon gone,
Disappearing from the
High streets,
Something's wrong.

3. Barristers

When you think about it,
It's all down to the brief;
A voice of reason
Common sense
To unravel the grief

Prosecute or defend?
Evidence to make a case.
Sharp-minded, sharp tongue
Is evidence in place?

Cross-examination and question
Witnesses lie;
Win over the sympathy
Of the jury,
Catch the judge's eagle eye

Advocate's final words
Judge's summing up speech
Jury's unanimous verdict
Guilty or to be released?

4. Estate Agents

One per cent, two per cent
Sometimes even more,
A share of your house
Your land and your front door

Moving pictures of all the rooms,
Measurements to be exact,
Exaggeration of marketing
It's all a matter of fact

Up goes the board
High price valuation,
Everyone now knows your
Business and location

Viewers in dribs and drabs
Time-wasters galore,
Still no interested buyers?
It's been three months or more!

Reduction in valuation
Market's now in decline,
Right on the money
Told them all the time

Sale now completed
Board's been taken down,
Middleman – a piece of cake
For sending a buyer around

5. Insurance Underwriters

You never get to see
These cool, calculating minds
You're a name, a number,
A liability, until you
Can prove otherwise

They weigh you right up
Treat you as a past statistic,
Provide you with quotations
Never taking a gamble or risk

You take your choice
You pay your money,
Expect in return
Pages of gobbledegook,
Words in writing
That sounds funny

Excesses and exclusions
Legal jargon in small print,
Try making a claim –
It's all the same.
Makes you read and think

No-claims bonus
No-blame claims
The underwriters control
The profit margins
By doing simple things,
Increasing the excess
And premiums paid.

6. Politicians

Party allegiance
Career ambitions,
Morals and principles
Serious decisions

Promise the world
Pretend to listen,
Convincing speeches
Manifesto vision

Take a stand
Take the flak,
Pit your wits
Watch your back

MPs on TV
Ranting and raving,
Who wants what?
Political bantering

Back bench
Front bench
Recognition and fame,
Honour or lies?
The political game

7. Publicity Agents

They're about grabbing the headlines
Spinning things around a lot
Exploiting all the media avenues
For clients who are successful – or not

They're about making mountains out of molehills,
Turning water into honey,
Elaborating stories about individuals
For the public to buy to make money

Bad news is good news!
To generate stories of public interest
They jump on to the bandwagon
Craving to know everything about
Their lives and success

If celebrities are on the up
They build up their reputation and luck,
Branding products in their name
Superstar status with all the fame

If celebrities careers nosedive
They reinvent them: what a surprise!
Promote them into soap and reality TV
Into the limelight to earn their money

8. Publishers

Publisher's commercial eye
Will test the author
To give it another try
May be worth another look
Could have the potential to become
A successful book

Readers are inclined
To read a bestseller,
Those others have tried.
Interest and value
Come first,
Followed by flowing words
Into chapter and verse

Publisher's creative mind
Knows what process it takes
To promote the lines;
Looking for literature that's new
Seeking out a bestseller
That comes out of the blue

9. Solicitors

Nothing seems black
Nothing looks white –
Nothing is quite simple
Or quite right

The book of knowledge
I have learned to explore,
Gives me the right
To uphold the law

Trust me to read
In between the lines,
You can depend I will defend
With my legal mind

Sue for all words
And deeds wrongly done,
Instigate proceedings
For justice to be won

Settle out of court
See you in the dock;
Charge by the minute
Until the clock stops

10. Stockbrokers

City slickers
Computer twitters
Crazy traders
Profit-takers

Opinions and numbers
Rewards and risks
Market spread analysis
Portfolio blue chips

Commodities and indices
Bonds and shares
Ups and downs
Paper millionaires

Crash, bang, wallop
Shares nosedive
Panic selling
Speculators buy

Headaches and palpitations
Buy, sell and hold
Frantic trading days
Buy into gold!